THE ORIGINAL INDESTRUCTIBLES®

For ages 0 and up!

Books babies can really sink their gums into!

Can you wiggle your *toes*? Now kick your *feet*!
Reach up and touch—it's your *nose*!
Time to close your *eyes*. Sleep tight, baby!
Learn all the parts of your body with
a book that's INDESTRUCTIBLE.

DEAR PARENTS: High-Color, High-Contrast INDESTRUCTIBLES nurture your baby's developing eyesight. And they're built for the way babies "read": with their hands and mouths. INDESTRUCTIBLES won't rip or tear and are 100% washable. They're made for baby to hold, grab, chew, pull, and bend.

CHEW ALL THESE AND MORE!

Copyright © 2022 by Indestructibles, LLC. Used under license. Illustrations copyright © 2022 by Workman Publishing. All rights reserved. Library of Congress Cataloging-in-Publication Data is available. Workman Kids is an imprint of Workman Publishing, a division of Hachette Book Group, Inc.

The Workman name and logo are registered trademarks of Hachette Book Group, Inc.

Distributed in the United Kingdom by Hachette Book Group, UK, Carmelite House, 50 Victoria Embankment, London EC4Y 0DZ.

Distributed in Europe by Hachette Livre, 58 rue Jean Bleuzen, 92 178 Vanves Cedex, France.

Contact special.markets@hbgusa.com regarding special discounts for bulk purchases.

All INDESTRUCTIBLES books have been safety-tested and meet or exceed ASTM-F963 and CPSIA guidelines.

INDESTRUCTIBLES is a registered trademark of Indestructibles, LLC.

Cover © 2024 Hachette Book Group, Inc.
First Edition April 2022 | 10 9 8 7 6 5 4 3
Printed in China | IMFP

$5.99 US / $7.99 Can.
ISBN 978-1-5235-1591-2

WORKMAN PUBLISHING • Hachette Book Group, Inc., 1290 Avenue of the Americas, New York, NY 10104 • indestructiblesinc.com